For Wally

Come before Winter

Reflections on Faith and the Indomitable Spirit
of Man and Nature

Come before Winter

Reflections on Faith and the Indomitable Spirit of Man and Nature

Poems by

Jo Taylor

© 2024 Jo Taylor. All rights reserved.
This material may not be reproduced in any form, published,
reprinted, recorded, performed, broadcast,
rewritten or redistributed without
the explicit permission of Jo Taylor.
All such actions are strictly prohibited by law.

Cover design by Shay Culligan
Cover image by Arūnas Naujokas on Unsplash
Author photo by Kayla Beckworth Photography

ISBN: 978-1-63980-513-6

Kelsay Books
502 South 1040 East, A-119
American Fork, Utah 84003
Kelsaybooks.com

Notes and Acknowledgments

My heartfelt thanks to Faith Shearin for reading many of the poems in this collection, for suggestions and encouragement, for her own poems that have spoken to me over the years; to Rosemerry Wahtola Trommer for facilitating classes during COVID, classes which gave me confidence and put me on the path to writing; to Lorette Luzajic at *The Ekphrastic Review* for publishing many of my early works. And to Cortney Wade, who encouraged me all the way, who laughed and cried with me over the stories shared and the lessons learned, thank you for "coming before winter" to see your dad and me through the hardest season of our lives.

I also thank the editors of the following journals or presses where my poems first appeared, sometimes in earlier versions:

Agape Review: "Asses and Angel Wings," "Things to Do to Take Heart," "Stouthearted," "Pitching the A," "Freefall," "To Come to Nought"

Blue Heron Review: "Dixie Landing"

The Ekphrastic Review: "Reflections on My Legacy After Visiting the Ramses Exhibit at the Natural Museum of the Arts in Houston," "Witnesses," "On Andrew Wyeth's *Public Sale, 1943*"

Georgia Poets Society's *Reach of Song* (2022): "A Cento on Living"

Heart of Flesh Literary Journal: "What My Sister Taught Me," "Conviction"

Local Gems Press, Chapbooks: "Adapting in 2021," "Come before Winter," "On Pruning," "Spelunking," "The Path at Sixty-Seven," "The Life Giver," "Evening"

MockingHeart Review: "Complicity," "Does Anyone Ever Realize Life While They Live It?" "Awaiting the Phoebe's Song"

Nebraska Poetry Society: "grandma mable"
One Art: "The Heart"
Poets on Line: "How to Warm Hearts and Ease Relationships," "After Reading Guthrie's 1946 New Year's Resolutions," "Eye-Openers"
Reformed Journal: "On Leaping," "Passover Donkey," "Triolet on Holding On," "On Hardships," "I Am Waiting," "Juxtaposition"
Silver Birch Press: "Over the Low Flame"
Snapdragon: A Journal of Art and Healing: "Fog Basking," "Of These I Sing"
Verse-Virtual: "Joy Unspeakable," "Monotony," "Melancholia in Deep Autumn," "Forgiveness," "Now," "Recollections on the Burning of Our House, 1980," "Making Do," "A Study of Hands," "Marrow and Mutation," "Ode to the Fruitcake," "Behold!"

"I Am Waiting" references Marie Durand, Huguenot prisoner in the Tour de Constance in the 18th century, story accessed online at *Musée Protestant.*

The "masters" alluded to in the subtitle and referenced in italics in "Lines Written in UAB's Bone Marrow Transplant Unit, 8423," refer to Shakespeare, Rosemerry Wahtola Trommer, The Bible, Barbara Crooker, and Rosemerry Wahtola Trommer, in that order.

Contents

Spring

On Leaping	17
Joy Unspeakable	18
Blast	19
Pain and Glory	20
Heralders of Hope	21
Patience	22
Asses and Angel Wings	23
Because	24
On Pruning	25
Reflections on My Legacy After Visiting the Ramses Exhibit at the Natural Museum of the Arts in Houston	26
Joy, Speakable	27
Death and Dust	28
Villanelle for Sister's Memorial Service, April 10, 2022	29
Passover Donkey	30
Complicity	32
Through the Glass, Darkly	34
What I Remember	35
Triolet on Holding On	36
How to Warm Hearts and Ease Relationships	37
A Cento on Living	38

Summer

Monotony	41
Spelunking	42
To Know the Mystery,	43
What My Sister Taught Me	44
Adapting in 2021	45

Still Life with Apron	46
grandma mable	47
Fog Basking	48
Things to Do to Take Heart	49
Dixie Landing	50
Summer of '69	51
The Path at Sixty-Seven	52
After Reading Guthrie's 1946 New Year's Resolutions	53
Does Anyone Ever Realize Life While They Live It?	54
Song of Summer	55
Sunday Morning Gospel	56
Of These I Sing	58
On Hardships	60

Autumn

Melancholia in Deep Autumn	63
1969, When My Mother Worked as a Nanny	64
Forgiveness	66
Over the Low Flame	67
Recollections on the Burning of Our House, 1980	68
So Much Depends	69
Making Do	70
Stouthearted	71
Conviction	72
Pitching the A	74
A Study of Hands	75
October Storms	76
I Am Waiting	77
Transplant Day	78
Freefall	79

Lines Written in UAB's Bone Marrow Transplant Unit, 8423	80
Sanctuary	82

Winter

Juxtaposition	85
Old Coffers,	86
Eye-Openers	87
Marrow and Mutation	90
Tilt-o-Whirl World	91
Witnesses	92
Because Life Is So Full of Music—I Shall Dance	93
Master Class	94
After November Frost	96
Making Candy in December	97
Christmas Across the Years	98
Ode to the Fruitcake	100
Family Gathering, December 17, 2022	102
I Walk the Path	103
On Andrew Wyeth's *Public Sale,* 1943	104
Déjà Vu	105
Truth and Beauty	106
The Working Dead	108
Awaiting the Phoebe's Song	109
The Heart	110
To Come to Naught	111
On Suffering	112
The Life-Giver	113
Evening	114
Now	115
Behold!	116
Proclamations in Fire and Ice	117
Come before Winter,	118

*Make every effort to come to me soon . . .
Try your best to come before winter.*
—2 Timothy 4:9,21 (AMP)

Spring

On Leaping

I want to leap like a raging fire,
like the lame man who was healed,
to thrill and bound with gazelles and goats
on mountaintops and in the plains.
I want to pop with springtime color,
to sing with frogs and beluga whales,
to jump with dolphins and white-tailed deer,
as I go about my day. I want to romp
with the desert mouse in moonlight
and gallop with wild horses at dawn.
I want to flit with the perky blue jay
and to frolic with the leopard at play.
Oh, Lord, allow me to skip with joy,
to dance with delight, to know in full
how much the heart can hold.

Joy Unspeakable

A small quaint town along the eastern shores
of Mobile Bay in mid-April, flowering baskets
of yellow and blue
                      suspended
from wrought-iron columns lining the cobbled streets.
Oh, the joy!

A cozy bistro with French flair, fresh
ruby roses gracing white linen cloths,
young waiters, formal, their beauty
accessorized in red bow ties, serving up
crawfish beignets, lobster quiche and crème brûlée.
Oh, the joy!

And the two of us here in the corner,
perhaps in this brief hour, subjects for art.
Paint us in detail, with strokes, delicate or harsh
or create us big and three-dimensional, in whole or in part,
but capture our bliss, frieze our delight,
when time was
                      suspended
like flowers in springtime.
Oh, the joy!

Blast

. . . they (words) can be cruel or kind,
and they can change their meanings right in front of you.
—John Steinbeck

Language, alive and changing.
Take the word *blast,* for instance,
an Old English word meaning
a blowing, a breeze, a puff of wind.
Today we speak of the *blast* we had
at Bible school or at Grandma's or
on our Mediterranean cruise or
at Saturday's tailgate party,
or we talk of a boss's *blasting*
an employee for his performance
or lack thereof or NASA's new moon
rocket *blasting* off at Cape Canaveral,
or the *blast* of color on the horizon.
We hear sirens *blast* in the neighborhood,
we send a *blast* of emails, we experience
a *blast* from the past upon hearing
The Eagles' soft-rock, six-minute
title track, *Hotel California.* And
just today, I learn of yet another
meaning, sinister, involving you
and blizzarding through my heart
like a *blast* of Arctic air. *Blast*—
abnormal, immature, out-of-control,
white blood cells impeding other
cells necessary for life.

19

Pain and Glory

—after W. H. Auden

We are born to suffer, to groan. And we go it
alone. Hear the refrain in the works of the Old
Masters, in their depictions of Icarus' fall
from the heavens, of the martyrdom of the saints,
of the suffering servant on the hillside near Jerusalem,
the world hardly noticing the whisper, *Eloi! Eloi!
Lama sabachthani.* Ask a country taking on the armies
of a tyrant-madman, its women and children displaced,
its elderly at the mercies of strangers. Yes, the Masters
got it right over five hundred years ago—or did they?
Consider me and mine on this maddening day in March
as sorrow advances in battalions, bombarding our tents
like missiles of war, yet see our doctors seeking out
new treatments, an international organ donor responding
to our call for help. Consider the animal world, the elephants
tossing dust on the wounds of their companions, their trunks
plucking tranquilizing darts set deep into their fellow tuskers.
Consider the gentle rain showing up to mourn with you
as you lay your family member to his final rest.

Heralders of Hope

—after news of a life-altering disease

arriving in spring's white
blossoming groundcover
and other creeping greens
tenderly trailing the worn gray
fence; in the cherry's pink
clusters in the cruellest month;
in the wood thrush's haunting
dawn song, flute-like, ethereal;
in the days' lengthening like salt-
water taffy, pulled and stretched
and thinned in a child's hands.

Patience

In the waiting room—
It is all about the odds

Hope suspended in air—
Like red cells
In the blood

The examining cubicle, cold—
The wall painting's sword-like crocosmia
Drooping

Paleness settling in—
Like a collection
Of milk glass

Bodies, rusting from the inside—
Old cars in boneyards

Voices and skin thinning—
Like patience

Asses and Angel Wings

You've spoken through donkeys, burning
bushes, wall writings, and even blood.
You have whispered, you have shouted,
you have called us by name. So today,
Lord, speak, in whatever medium you choose,
and, pray, O God, do not let us miss the message.
Speak through the yellow-beaked, orange-breasted,
not-so-shy robin, flitting about our feet
in the infirmary gardens; through the scurrying,
red-tailed fox squirrel, peeking from the forked limbs
of the sclerotic live oak as if to say I am
worth the camera; through the pink and white crepe
myrtles, their papery, cinnamon-colored, sometimes
leprosy-looking, trunks gracing entrances
to the medical buildings; and in the newly-flowering
redbuds, purpling with passion. Speak through
the flutter of angel wings, the silence of stars,
through the chaos of sickness, through
the soft sinking sun. You who have made us,
and not we ourselves, come and commune
with your people. We confess we know not
why you will and how you will, but that you will.

Because

yesterday a stranger stopped and tied your shoe
on your morning walk in the neighborhood; because

in the sanctuary that Sunday morning when your pearly whites
sported lipstick laughingly and loud, a visitor signaled to you

in a heavenly language to lick your teeth and to keep right on
singing; because umpteen cards and text messages, invisible

hugs and kisses from home, moused their way under the door
every day during a five-week stay at the nation's top cancer

institute; because a passenger, doused with sleep in the seat
beside you on your flight home, awakened just in time

to retrieve luggage from the overhead bin, pausing
a moment to say *you have beautiful eyes*

On Pruning

Master Gardener, Heavenly Vinedresser,
Lord of the Harvest, be gracious to me

and embolden me with bright hues and warm
colors; stretch forth your hand and examine

my foliage to see if there be parasites sucking away
at my life, old habits, worldly thoughts,

perhaps untethered pride. Take away the overgrowth
that is arrogance, the undergrowth that is gluttony,

envy and greed, all the excesses keeping out the light.
Revive and renew, cut and prune, and if it hurts,

help me through the pain and allow me a glimpse
of the bumper crop you are producing. Grow me

to your specifications; hold not your good gifts
from me. On second thought, Lord—

maybe I could do with a little less color, a tad
fewer hues.

Reflections on My Legacy After Visiting the Ramses Exhibit at the Natural Museum of the Arts in Houston

—to my husband, who was recently diagnosed with a rare and debilitating disease

Today, I am thinking about my legacy,
what I can hope for, what I might achieve.
I will never be a Beethoven, a Mozart, a Picasso
or a Keats, will never be crowned with an olive
wreath nor TikTok my way to fame. I won't be
in the annals of history or in the research journals
of science or in the exhibits of great pharaohs,
whose cartouche carvings and jewelry collections
blazon the family tombs of their mighty empires
like a jillion coral polyps underneath the surface
of the sea. But what I could achieve is a good name,
one chiseled in a single stone, a name suggesting
a rock or a gracious giver or one who has withstood
great heat. A name like Shadrack, a name like yours.

Joy, Speakable

—for Dr. V. on April 4, 2022, upon our learning of approval of trial drug

The news arrives like morning's
freshly baked bread. Approved—
for life-quickening, hope-infused,
courage-forging physic.
Straightaway, neon displays
shoo away the gray day, and
marketplace's morning glories
open miraculously to song.

Death and Dust

—April 9, 2022, on the death of a sibling

Death,
just a momentary halt
in the dark, just a pause
for the Light to show up
and swaddle you for the euphoric
journey through galaxies and stars
and the Milky Way. How is it
The Creator regards mere dust?

Villanelle for Sister's Memorial Service, April 10, 2022

—after Fain and Kahal

We will see you in the summer's ferns, in fall's colors and its chill
In birthday cards, in a hand that penned, with love and thought and care
We'll hear you in the river, raging, in its waters, calm and still.

We will look for you in the plight of children, in injustice, imagined, real
We will find you with the lonely, in places cold and cruel and bare
We will see you in the summer's ferns, in fall's colors and its chill.

You'll be there in the things of Christmas, in its trees, décor, and meal
In all the family socials, in our gatherings now more rare
We'll hear you in the river, raging, in its waters calm and still.

In the April rains we'll see you, in the gentle breeze, we'll feel
We'll find you playing in the dirt or at antique marts and fairs
We will see you in the summer's ferns, in fall's colors and its chill.

We'll look for you, dear sister, in the mountains, fields, and hills
And we know that you will be there as we seek and search where'er
We'll hear you in the river, raging, in its waters calm and still.

We will see you in the good and bad of our time here, so until
We meet again, our precious one, in dreams or in the air
We will see you in the summer's ferns, in fall's colors and its chill
We'll hear you in the river, raging, in its waters, calm and still.

Passover Donkey

*Behold, your King is coming to you; He is just and having salvation,
lowly and riding on a donkey, a colt, the foal of a donkey*
—Zechariah 9:9

Little donkey of Bethany, foretold
in holy writ, you were born for this
moment. Tell me, do you feel His sobs

as you plod toward Jerusalem? Do you
tear, too? Are you aware of the drag
of His body, as the path grows steeper,

more treacherous, the rocks cutting
into your tender feet? Do you struggle
to stay close behind your mother, fearful

of a misstep, anxious over the mob's pushing
and shoving and invading your space,
their clamor reverberating across the mountain

with a pitch and fever to awaken the dead?
Do you feel the breeze from the palm fronds?
An occasional sting on your youthful skin?

Are you smitten with the children, suffering
them near you, their evergreens and voices,
sweet, strewn along the path, *Hosanna,*

Hosanna, Hosanna in the Highest.
Surely, little beast of burden, your legs tremble
and your heart quivers—for upon the back

of the One you carry will soon rest the weight
of the world. Upon His back, the wrath of God.

Complicity

It touts my first date, the Prom of '71.
The day was not particularly memorable
except for the anticipation I felt leading
up to the event, for my date, gifted
by my brother, was surely the most
coveted prince in our little kingdom,
a tall, blue-eyed blonde about six-
and-a-half feet tall. He picked me up
in his sports coupe, and we exchanged niceties,
pinned carnations onto each other's breasts,
and drove the short distance to the private
festivities where we smiled for camera
and administration and sipped yellow fruit
punch like butterflies imbibing on the nectar
of phlox and buddleia and exchanged more
niceties with each other and with classmates.
If I remember correctly, I was home by eleven,
without so much as a kiss from the dashing
college senior in baby-blue tuxedo who had been
my escort for the evening.

Fifty years later my heart still languishes,
as I read yearbook entries from the class
of '71, not from my handsome prince
who might have stolen my heart away
on that warm Friday evening in early May,
but from two classmates of color
who had joined our class of twenty-five
when we were juniors. There in my annual
in beautiful pen are the words from the one
steeped in silence, the one sitting near
the windows on the last row of history class.

*Never forget that there's one boy who thinks
you are more special than special.* You got it
wrong, E, you got it wrong. I didn't fight for you
to join the party. I left you sitting there
in that last row of history class, lost
in your dreams. Today, I search for you,
but you are already gone. Today, I carry the weight
of your words, the weight of my silence.

Through the Glass, Darkly

I remember the evening in springtime,
the auditorium redolent with gardenias,
sawdust, and chatter, the rows
of dark walnut seats with ornate cast-iron
anchored to floor, him in his khaki-best
trousers and Sunday resoled and
polished black slippers, waiting
for curtain to rise, hands clasped,
thumbs rotating like windmills. But
she was not there. She was not a part
of the pageantry. She would not see
her daughter at the baby grand, fingering
the ivories under bright stage lights. She
would not smile as her seventh child
glided across the stage in yellow sequined
gown and white satin shoes nor feel heart-
skips at audience's applause when the master
of ceremonies called her girl's number
to advance in the competition. Was her
absence due to apathy? Fatigue? Pride?
Maybe she was principled against pageants,
thought them silly, demeaning, cruel.
After five decades, though, I see her.
It's late at night. She's sitting at the Singer
sewing machine after a long day's work.
She's taking in darts in the yellow dress,
measuring, marking and stitching, moving,
at last, to the ironing board to flatten
the bulk and set the stitches, ensuring
the hand-me-down formal the perfect
fit for her daughter's debut. I see her
clearly. She was there.

What I Remember

—after Lucille Clifton

about that Saturday in early spring
is a bloat of people, like harpy-eagles
on the hunt, the sun rising over the flower
garden, long in ruins, broken clay pots
and earthen statues scattered across
the barren soil, fish pool overrun
with slugs and moss and slime.
Just stacks of dishes and thin,
fire-worn pots and pans cluttering kitchen
counter. And drawers of silverware, cutlery,
and odds and ends, all open for scavenging.
And us aproned with our money bags
and plastic and paper bags, flitting here
and there, negotiating prices. *I'll take
five dollars for that piece of Waterford.
A buck-fifty? But it was a retirement gift
thirty years ago. Okay, then, a buck-fifty—
we've only a day to get this done. It's yours.
And that beautiful frame you're holding,
the one with the service award, free.
Take it. Nowhere to store the stuff.*
No talk that day of her fondness for pretty
things, nothing about demise of family,
once virulent and strong.

Triolet on Holding On

Take heart—
they say the darkest hour gives birth to light,
the pain and pitch and fog, saliva-thick, but then, the brand-new start.
Take heart—
joy comes with the resting of the ark,
light breaking, waters receding, squalls and winds withdrawn.
Take heart—
the darkest hour gives birth to light.

How to Warm Hearts and Ease Relationships

Invite the stony heart to go with you
to fish for crappie in April. Pure fun.

No fancy equipment needed. A cane pole
and minnows work just fine. Find a cove and

anchor near shoreline's brush piles or cypress
or troll alongside an old log jetting out

into the shallows. Give a good cast
and be patient. A crappie seldom strikes

with gusto so be on your mark for the hit.
When you feel the pull, set the hook

with a gentle tug upward so you don't tear
its paper-thin mouth. If you have bad luck,

turn your pockets inside out or ease on over
to another spot and try again, enjoying

the warm sun on your face and shoulders.
Continue for a good part of the day. Know

there's no pressure to catch a mess
because you can always make up a tale

to tell your friends back home, but if
you catch a string of 'em, go ashore and

fry 'em up for a meal fittin' and fillin'.
Besides that, anything can happen

near water during the breaking of bread.
An atrophied heart might even feel a tug.

A Cento on Living

We are dust and dreams;
we live in what kills us.
We are put on earth a little space
       that we may learn to bear the beams of love,
       to leave tracks.
Somehow, each of us will help the other live, and somewhere,
       each of us must help the other die—
golden lads and girls all must, as chimney-sweepers, come to dust;
so teach us to number our days,
       that we may apply our hearts unto wisdom.

Line 1: A.E. Housman
Line 2: John N. Morris
Lines 3–4: William Blake
Line 5: Ruth Bader Ginsburg
Lines 6–7: Adrienne Rich
Line 8: William Shakespeare
Lines 9–10: Psalm 90:12 (KJV)

Summer

Monotony

Beachballs as colorful as the flower-hat jelly fish
and carried by the wind; gulls, gray, white and black,

screeching like a stainless-steel knife against beer bottle
and competing for crumbs around the abandoned

lounge chair; airplanes bannering *Best Parasailing
Guaranteed;* pull-carts hauling tents and towels and

little tots; white sand pocked with a million footprints,
dunes and craters here and there, sometimes a castle

doomed to wed with water; the young, tanned and
bronzed, playing frisbee, some showing off

their full-bodied, labyrinthine tattoos, others
with a single design, but all slathered in shine

to pay homage to the sun god; the old, tummies
protruding like a frog's goozle, wading

at water's edge, searching for shells, or resting
under umbrellas and behind dark glasses; a loud

speaker expanding the sounds of a couple's
iPhone playlist, the two facing each other, inching

closer, then touching, then embracing, we breathing
their sweetness; waves lapping the shore and

retreating time and time again, their monotony fresh,
like new tongues.

Spelunking

Life, like navigating a cave—
maneuvering through rocky formations,

adjusting to light and dark, cautiously
maintaining good footing

on slippery terrain, carefully
observing low-hanging dripstones,

their rivals stretching upwards,
further complicating twists and turns

and tight squeezes. And the bats! O,
the bats! But then—in the innermost caverns,

a lake, blue, spectacular, soulful, rising up
to greet you, like calm, like contentment,

like an exhale.

To Know the Mystery,

—after Wendell Berry

explore the mysterious.
Step into the darkness

and feel your way,
inching from fear to joy,

from trepidation to pride.
Inch to the edge

of the precipice
like a child advancing

first time to diving board's
jumping off point,

and feel time stop
and breathing halt

that afterwards
you know the heartbeat

of a thousand kettle drums.

What My Sister Taught Me

Take It to the Limit One More Time
                —The Eagles

She taught me to rumba, to pick a partner from the crowd,
to coax him to the floor, to move carefree and wild, like water
on a hot griddle, laughing all the while. She taught me to show up

and show off. To star. (Even in family photographs, she stood out,
her dark corkscrew curls, her big brown eyes, playful, inviting,
her charisma coloring the card stock.) She taught me big. Big

hair, big ideas, big heart. To climb into bed with the dying,
to stroke their faces, to caress with kisses even when the verdict
is out on the disease's power to transmit. She taught me to fancy

mustard greens and collards and Krispy Kreme and Diet Coke.
To believe in yourself when, like an exploding soda can,
the world spits and spews *no, can't, impossible, it won't happen*

and then to watch the miracle manifest itself a thousand times
in a tiny village in Africa or in the heart of a special needs
teenage son. She taught me to borrow a sister's panties and

to suffer the consequences. To croon Patsy Cline, recording
yourself at Six Flags or in make-shift home studio. To commune
with The Creator on the beach when life barrels toward you,

the container heavy with loss and grief. She taught me to care and
care and then to care a little more. Because loss had opened her
to love.

Adapting in 2021

Today, I am stripping
down, ridding
myself of anger
angst and shame,
converting
today's roofless,
flared-wheel,
shiny-red
speedster
to the Bennett Buggy
of the thirties,
the Hoover Wagon
of yesterday. I am
loading up that old
windowless,
engine-free,
mule-carted
vehicle
with gratitude,
thanksgiving,
generosity and love,
fueling myself
with faith,
acceptance,
mercy, grace, and love.
Repurposed, relieved,
I am easing on
down the road.

Still Life with Apron

Bibbed about neck and tied around
belly full from decades of child-
bearing, our mother's homespun-
cotton apron, pocketed; flour-dusted
by the biscuit-making in morning,
at mid-day and again at evening; worn
from toting many-a mess of peas,
pickings of fresh, off-the-vine, blood-
ripe tomatoes, an egg or two scooped from
straw on the way past the chicken coop.
It is hot pad, tear-catcher, nose-wiper,
and protector-of-dress. It pockets
safety pins and pennies, screws, and nuts
and bolts. At the close of day, it's a still-life
resting on the big poster bed—buckets
of yellow flowers on French country toile
or Dorothy-blue gingham trimmed in red
rick rack, or a mercy-filled, white muslin field,
grace gracing the entire landscape.

grandma mable

—after Lucille Clifton

when i think of you
in your fuzzy-pink, faux-fur bedroom slippers
limping like you had long wrestled with jacob's angel
lighting up and taking a drag of your carefully-crimped prince
albert, the smoke circling above your head like a fading
sensuousness

when i think of you
running a comb through your tired, wavy-thick hair, hoary
like ocean's spew against the muted sea sand
planting a pinch of snuff between your lower gum and cheek
as you scurry about shooing cats nestled in your worn easy-chair
or on the kitchen counter

when i think of you
chauffeuring the folks to doctors and diviners
or crocheting blankets for grandbabies and old men
your arthritic hands crimped like rita hayworth pin-curls
your failing eyesight as dim as the speakeasies of your girlhood

when i think of the cortege
escorting you to the gardens of your final resting place
monument-still policemen holding at attention as the hearse rolls
by, strangers in their automobiles yielding a moment
for your hundred-plus years, your black-veiled sons and daughters
processing solemn and staid

i light up o daughter of zeus child of eurynome i light up

Fog Basking

This week after rejection slips as plentiful
as book titles in the Library of Congress's
online catalog, I turn to the darkling beetle
in the dry habitats of our world, his legs
pinching forward an inch at a time
to find drink, to bask in the early morning
dew, in the fog atop desert dunes rising
in the distance like Mt. Everest; to harvest
the water droplets in pits and crevices
of his back; to stand on his head in mist
and wind, opening his mouth for trickles,
refreshing himself for the journey home.

Oh, to be that thirsty. To go the distance.
To find life in your own cisterns,
in your own bumps and fractures.

Things to Do to Take Heart

Learn nature's names—identify columbine
and catmint, Orion and Taurus. Take note

of the toadstool, the miraculous little fairy cap
springing up before dawn, burnt-orange, under-gilled

domes on slender, slick stalks muting their way to light.
Play in the dirt. Plant a garden with cucumbers,

radishes, zucchini, and peas—white acre and purple
hull—for their contrasting soups dueling it out

on winter's hearth. Wouldn't hurt to scatter some
flower seeds when you break the ground, too—

nothing like sunflowers to dress up a field in summer.
Listen to the swinging spirituals album gifted

by your six-months friend or better yet, hear her
singing *Swing Down Jericho* at the surgical center

or Hospice house where she volunteers. Like her,
make the best of every opportunity for doing good—

compliment the Uber driver, the mail carrier,
grocery's checkout girl or better yet, become an organ

donor. Make a Spiderman cake with your grandsons,
allowing the mixer to sling red and blue cake batter

on walls, in hair, in memories. Read a poem, write
a poem, with the kids and for them, but mostly for you.

Crank out a churn of vanilla bean ice cream and invite
your neighbor over to celebrate summer. At day's end,

bow the knee and lean into the difficulty of the hour.

Dixie Landing

From town, go down the paved road towards Johnson's
Chapel for two miles until the road makes a sharp turn
to the right, a large, white farm house in the bend,

turn left on a dirt road through brambles and overgrown
bushes until the air grows cooler and then drive
a few hundred feet past overhanging limbs and branches

stinging with new life and there, when the road ends,
you'll find Dixie Landing, a swimming hole with cool,
unemotional water and turtles on logs getting what little sun

they can find in the naked light, where the moon feels
challenged in its rendezvous with its mirrored friend during
the nighttime, where a verdant foliage invites kingfishers and

lacey, translucent-winged dragonflies and butterflies, and twisted
primeval cypress entices teens to swing from its ropes far out
over the water.

Summer of '69

It was a hum-drum existence, the summer
of '69. We stood in tiny cubicles eight hours
a day buttoning newly manufactured shirts,
folding and tucking this way and that, compressing
for packaging and shipping. Day-in, day-out, we
stretched and tugged and pulled and pinched to make
garments pucker and wrinkle-free, earning money
for our bell bottoms, leather vests, tie-dyes, and
class rings. Nothing extraordinary that summer
except Dylan and Joplin, Hendrix and The Doors
and that one day in early June when we rushed
during lunch like the lava at Pompeii to tune the car's
radio to our local staticky station. We held our breath.
Would your number come up? If so, could you be
deferred? Would you be numbered among the lucky?

I heard after your tour in Nam you continued to battle
the night, writhing, twisting, fetaling into the darkness,
your screams curdling even the stars. And when I learned
of your fateful fall from the rooftop a few years later,
I thought about our mundane lives that summer of '69.
How fresh we were then, not yet weary with life's furrows
and folds, its creases, its lines.

The Path at Sixty-Seven

—inspired by the gardens of J and D

Observe how the lilies of the field grow; they do not toil nor do they spin, yet I say to you that even Solomon in all his glory did not clothe himself like one of these.
—Matt. 6:28–29 NASB

From the computer to the dock, I glory
in purples and blues, the petunias and salvia
stretching toward the light, in stipple,
mint-green holly, in hydrangeas, brown,
drying artfully in the extravagant summer sun.
I laud the climbing sunflower creeping along
trellis, its bright face inviting me to join the party,
the yellow and black swallow-tail butterfly
urging me to lead the dance. I turn back
at the maddening sounds of the cicada and then
the lone bird hidden high in the pines, mocking
playfully the insect's harsh tone. I want to play, too,
to empty self, to spin and stretch and sway and
make noises. I want to loosen up, to know myself
like the crickets know themselves, like bare apple
trees and wild and waxy leathery ferns, like
the tiny purple pods of the pine in springtime.

After Reading Guthrie's 1946 New Year's Resolutions

You could listen to his songs and actually learn how to live.
—Bob Dylan

I've loved you for a quarter-century,
you, singing of see-through tater stew, you,
speaking for the working man and woman,
you, giving us voice and hope
in your three-thousand songs and ballads,
you, who took us riding in your car
and put us on the train bound for glory.

                          I, who share
your July birthday, want to learn your way.
Show me how to live, to hobo across this land
hanging out under bridges and in tent cities,
among people whose dreams have morphed
into nightmares, among shoeless children,
paining for food, whose eyes have circled
and darkened and caved like sinkholes.
Teach me to look into those kids' eyes and see
myself. Teach me to *stay glad* and *dream good*
and to *play good* and *sing good* and *to love.*
To *love everybody.* To *wake up every day* and *fight.*
Fight through injustice and prejudice,
through raging fires and bad luck, through fate and
tragedy as big as insane asylums, even when
I don't feel at home in this world anymore.

Does Anyone Ever Realize Life While They Live It?

—after Thornton Wilder

Did I brush my teeth this morning? Take
my medicine? Change my underwear?

How do people fall in love? Out of love?
And if they fall out, were they ever really in?

What is the difference between forgiveness
and reconciliation?

When you learn there are 100 billion galaxies
each one containing a hundred billion stars,

do you feel boundless, immeasurable, or do you
feel constrained and small? What was life like

for Lazarus after returning to this side of paradise?
What was going on in his head as he stumbled out

of the grave? Thoreau said he did not want to live
a life that was not life, insisted he wanted to live

life deliberately. Did I notice, really notice,
the yellow-eyed grackle hopscotching at my feet

this morning? The bearded live oak, its arthritic arms
outstretched?

Song of Summer

Like as the waves make towards the pebbled shore
So do our minutes hasten to their end
—Shakespeare, Sonnet 60

Nothing like evening over water in late August,
the sunset creeping behind the horizon, a kaleidoscope
finaleing until out of sight; airplanes flying low,
the emerald calm flirting, inviting play
on its fickle surface; geese in perfect "V," signaling
the coming night and waning temperatures; children
at bow cuddled in towels at their mother's side and
lulled to dreams by engine's roar; and you and I,
life-jacketed at the back of the boat, aware of swells
around the bend, inching closer to each other
to soften the wave's impact, to lessen the looming chill.

Sunday Morning Gospel

I revel in this muggy, mid-July morning,
watching from the heavy, hammered-iron rocker

the oldest grand, his papa, and his mom and dad kick
the half-deflated ball, run the make-shift bases, laughter

resounding in the butterfly-filled and crepe myrtle-draped
back yard. I delight in the wrens and red birds on feeders, the large,

cracked and rusted dinner bell crowning the eight-foot pole
on which the hangers are anchored. I love the five-year-old's

water play, the baptisms he gives himself again and again,
the christening cool he allows me every now and then.

I take in the dozens of walkers out for a stroll this Sunday
morning before the sun reigns high in the sky, before

their Labs and Chihuahuas' tongues hang languid like lavender-
blue longing. And across the way, at the First Baptist Church,

the orchestra warms for their prelude of hymns, chaotic sounds
finally giving way to the beauty of *Teach me some melodious*

sonnet, sung by flaming tongues above. These tiny tremors in time,
momentous shocks of paradise. These fast flickers and glints,

enough joy for a lifetime.

Of These I Sing

—with lines from Walt Whitman and Robert Penn Warren

weekend drives with you to nowhere, at dawn or at dusk,
to discover poetry somewhere—by the meadow,
in the stream, in the skyline and in us

the miracle of motherhood, its mundane moments at the baseball
field, in school's drop-off line, at the bathroom sink, bringing
about the memorable, the monumental

those who believe without seeing

birthdays and anniversaries and graduations with bookoodles
of balloons; funerals, too, for *to die is different from what
any one supposed and luckier*

weddings—a blushing bride, a sweaty-palmed husband
and Pachelbel's *Canon in D*

freckled-faced little boys with plastic buckets, digging
for clams, chasing sandpipers, building castles in the air

high school students' hastily scribbled messages
of gratitude in meticulously bowed and rick-racked jelly jar

gifts in my life, gifts for my life, gifts of my life—friends

a thick, hearty potato soup in winter, sprinkled with freshly ground
black pepper and topped with sharp cheddar cheese and real bacon
bits, oyster crackers on the side

creek beds, tadpoles in eddies and streams

a flowing well on the outskirts of town, cool, refreshing
like a cloud burst in tobacco field in August's mid-afternoon
sizzling sun

the offerings of strangers, their nods, their waves,
their tips-of-hats, confirming our collective connection

words, words, words, except those from politicians

a hot, soaking, evening bath, hot enough to toughen
skin, relaxing enough to bring about sweet dreams of you

the time mankind will *love so well the world that we may
believe, in the end, in God.*

On Hardships

In the desert,
the tiny golden mole
swims across sand dunes,
paddling hard with broad claws.
He zips across the barren terrain,
like a tumbleweed,
diving deep now and then
to cool himself,
finally emerging
for another scoot.
What can he teach us,
this tiny creature of the dust?
Perhaps the answer lies
in the desolation, the thirst.

Autumn

Melancholia in Deep Autumn

Maybe it comes from the gray
clouds swirling fast in the heavens
like thoughts in a mother's head.
Perhaps it's the solitary crane soaring
low over sea or it's the bare apple tree
or the cherry, its leaves turning
a Midas-gold, a few florins now resting
upon the ground. Or is it the bird
house or the bath emptied of its warmth,
its chatter, its spray? Could it be
the coming on of winter?

1969, When My Mother Worked as a Nanny

When I was sixteen, my mother worked as maid and nanny for the town preacher and his educator wife. Nice people. Their house was up the street, a quarter mile from our place. Big, brick house, air conditioned, new.

One day my mother came home crying. Her employers would receive their salaries during upcoming holidays, but they would not pay hers. After staring at the floor for what seemed an eternity, she reconciled her fate. She would address the issue the next morning when her blood was not so warm.

My mother loved the reverend's children like they were her own. She thought she might work there a long time supplementing her house's income. She was raising the last of her nine, caring for a sick spouse, skimping, saving her pennies, for life's certain squeezes.

Within the hour, the reverend sat in our living room, wilted like summer's hydrangea, imploring my mother to return. She did. But not before I had felt her pride. Her hurt. Not before I had lost a measure of respect for two of my favorite teachers.

That night my mother scrubbed floors, ironed shirts and khakis, served our evening meal with a turbine's ferocity. The next day she left for work. Not long after, she walked back through the front door, this time, no tears. "I quit," she offered resolutely going about her household duties, less feverish this time.

Forgiveness

The mistake ninety-nine percent of humanity made, as far as facts could see, was being ashamed of what they were; lying about it, trying to be somebody else.
—J.K. Rowling

I remember attending the D.A.R.'s annual meeting
with my mother during my senior year, I, robed
in youth and the future and my mother's only pair
of run-free stockings, posing for the flashing cameras
and reporters, she in home-spun dress, austere and
unadorned, several years older than the other
mothers in the room, worn from days of carrying
the weight of work and ailing husband. I remember
accepting the school's Good Citizen award, ashamed—
ashamed of my poverty, ashamed of my mother's
primitiveness, ashamed of who I was. That night
I nestled deep in Mama's patched and piecemealed
quilt while the gold seal on the black framed certificate
blazed like Charon's eyes upon the dresser, exposing
a fraud.

Over the Low Flame

of the white-enameled cooktop nestled
in my auntie's cramped kitchen, a stew,
freshly-shucked oysters swimming in their milky liqueur

and seasoned with little pats of butter, a shake of salt,
and black pepper. O, the pepper freckling the delicacy
prepared especially for extended adult family's Saturday

supper. The women ladle the steaming gray-brown liquid
into large, orange-flowered bowls, the oysters curled
at edges and shriveled like shrinking dreams in the buttery,

flecked-with-flavor streams. Except for the slurp of soup
from serving-sized spoons, the men eat the meal in silence,
at length turning up bowl to down the last drop, ending

the meal with satisfying belch and back-of-hand swipe
across lips. In the meantime, the children finish
their white, light-bread-cloaked, condiments-choked wienies

and dash off to play as the women clear the table and
convene once more in the close quarters of the kitchen.

Recollections on the Burning of Our House, 1980

It was September. I remember my brother
beckoning me to the door of my classroom
to tell me our homeplace was burning.
I recall nothing much about our half-hour
drive to get there, but I must have been thinking
of the gathering room Daddy had carpentered
at the back of the house, one side wall and
the whole back wall windowed, curtained
just enough to allow in the sun and
a spectacular view of chickens pecking
in the yard near the rusty old barn and
buxom chinaberry tree. I must have thought
about our preparation of summer fruits and
vegetables on the front porch, the washing
of clothes on the back, Mama at work
in the kitchen, singing *Just a Little Talk
with Jesus.* And what of the physical items
that spoke of who we were? The mirrored,
whatnot-filled, upright piano hugging the
corner; the white, red-lettered, imitation-leather
Bible in oak bookcase; the shoeboxes brimming
with black and white photos, report cards
from our teachers, an occasional obituary clipping
from the local newspaper or advertisement
for Bantham or Leghorn chicks from the feed
and seed catalog. And though I must have thought
of the meeting we would hold to plan the support
and care of our mother, nothing could have prepared
me for the image when we turned onto the street,
the house a towering inferno. Standing in the middle
of the road, the citadel of our family, wringing
her hands, at times pulling her apron to her cheeks
to wipe the tears, whimpers, sometimes wails,
emanating from her core like a fawn in distress.

So Much Depends

—after William Carlos Williams

so much depends
upon
the free will
of man
working in tandem
with the
sovereign will
of God

Making Do

I see him even now, fixed on the task,
little golden tack pursed between lips,
hammer in right hand, another tack
in his left, straddling a rusty cast-iron
shoe form to re-sole our Sunday slippers.
I watch him measuring and cutting
the stiff leather square, fitting it
to the bottom of the shoe
from midway the sole to the toe,
the work as methodical and precise
as the earth's rotation, and then
securing it with tacks and tap,
tap, tap of the hammer. In those
moments he is god-like, showered
in the golden light of the twenty-five-
watt naked bulb suspended from ceiling.
Alone, he is making do. In the quietness
of the evening, he is articulating
the language of love.

Stouthearted

Be like the cliff against which the waves continually break;
but it stands firm and tames the fury of the water around it.
  —Marcus Aurelius

I've always thought myself stouthearted
not easily bruised, able to turn from those
who splinter the world with their hoary
wisdom and know-it-all pride, those
Job-like friends descanting about what
it means to live. But today I am faint,
tired of turning. I need something,
somebody, to teach me steadfastness
in the middle of the storm. Perhaps
the Great Basin Bristlecone Pine,
persevering through extreme conditions
to live thousands of years; scripture's
Mother Rizpah in the desert, keeping
a six-month vigil over the bodies
of her slain sons; the Golden Rule,
holding truth without turning or shadow.
Maybe Keats' lone star with its eternal lids
in the night sky or the sun moving through
the heavens in its dawn-to-dusk ritual or
the rocky cliff waiting, even inviting,
the thrashing waves.

Conviction

—after Margaret Atwood

All those times I was bored,
mind wandering, wandering,
many times out of the physical
space which was our living room
where he was on his knees in
the evenings, head bent, talking
more to the wooden floor
than to the Heavenly Father
he addressed, always pointing out
his shortcomings or pouring over
his guilt or begging for a cleansing
to make him Ivory Snow white.
I, too, bowed my head, lower,
lower into my lap, whispering
to myself, *enough, enough, please,
enough. You've reminded Him
already that He knows you,
your every thought, that He's
numbered the hairs on your now balding
head.* I count the carpet's hairs and the lines
in my palms and imagine the freckles
on the little finger of the one I would
one day marry. *One, two, three . . .
forty-nine, fifty, fifty-one.* Sometimes
the prayer warrior would speak
in a mysterious language, frightening,
yet musical, captivating, enticing,
like Handel's *Messiah,* and I would be
drawn back to his voice of steel and
see his face lifted, his arms, too,

communing with a world of which I was not
a part. Why do I remember the scene
more reverentially now, see him more
affectionately? I could not wait for the amen
when I would shake out my leg, long asleep,
and head fast to my room to read
Pride and Prejudice. Now I long for his
words of conviction and hunger for things
unseen.

Pitching the A

—in anticipation of my husband's bone marrow transplant one month out

I'd like to say I am petal-open
to the miracle October will bring,
but if truth be known, I am
like the fainting goat, stiffening,
seizing, even keeling over
from excitement and fear and dread.
I want to rush the hours to get to warm
days when your tired marrow surrenders
to new life. Yet, to hasten the moment
might mean missing out on the marvels
of today. So help me, Lord, even now,
to slow down, to be content with imagining
the smell of the birthday cake in the oven,
the sound of ice tinkling in the glasses,
the oboe pitching the A for orchestra's
warmup.

A Study of Hands

—for my husband, 2022

Science teaches that the hand's twenty-seven bones are controlled by thirty-seven muscles, that a quarter of the brain's motor cortex is dedicated to movement of the hand, from which five fingers

bend and stretch a quarter million times over a lifetime. But let's talk of your hands, the warm, sweaty-palmed, uncalloused hands that took my hand five decades ago as the vicar spoke of cleaving

'til death. Let's talk of your hard-working, attention-to-detail hands, changing the oil in the 1973 Ford Galaxy in our early years or laboring in pulp yards, in bakeries, on paint crews and cattle

farms to provide well for our family of two in young adulthood; or your strong hands, tugging and lifting and caressing an aged father, an invalid sister, a stranger bereft of hope after news

of child lost in the early days of the Iraqi War. Let's sing of loving, inviting, lighthearted hands patty-caking or itsy-bitsy-spidering with starry-eyed, six-month-old daughter. And then let's look

at your hands today, hands assaulted by chemotherapy, cracked and sensitive to heat and cold, fingers picked like well-worn wool, their nails bluing, lifting like asphalt shingles in September's

hurricane. Let's study the hands that have cupped grief and loss and joy and hope in the same moment.

October Storms

—to my husband, a week before stem cell transplant

Today we listen to Clapton's melancholic rendition
of *Autumn Leaves* and remote our way through news
and weather channels to learn more about the fury
of Hurricane Ian in the gulf, keenly aware
of the ensuing winter and the suffering our flesh
is heir to. In a few short days, you, too, will weather
the biggest storm of your life, and I will be helpless
to do anything about it. We will batten down
for forty and more days and wait for the wind to die
down and the squalls to subside that we might send out
the raven and dove to test the receding waters.

I Am Waiting

There is no greater harm than that of time wasted.
—Michelangelo

I am waiting for the traffic light to change, luck, too;
for someone to answer my phone call, to break into
the repetitive recording—*your waiting time is less than
thirty minutes.* I am waiting for the right opportunity.
I am waiting to lose weight, to sound like Lady Gaga,
to take her place alongside Tony Bennett. I am waiting
to find a bone marrow match for the love of my life
who's been with me nearly all my life.

                I recently read of a French woman
imprisoned thirty-eight years in the Tower of Constance
for practicing her faith. According to tradition, she became
her fellow prisoners' lifeline to the outside world, writing
letters to improve conditions in the dark, dank tower,
teaching her sisters to read and write and pass the time,
by watching her carve *Recistez* with her knitting needle
into the dungeon's stone wall.

I want to be like that woman. I want to wait *on*
while I wait *for*.

Transplant Day

for Christ plays in ten thousand places
         —Gerard Manley Hopkins

Every fall we make our way
to colorful festivals celebrating
the harvest—pumpkin festivals,
apple festivals, syrup-making
festivals—where we enjoy the cool,
mountain air as crisp as the apples
themselves, the warm, powdered-sugar
funnel cake, and the fresh Georgia
peanuts drawing revelers to the three-
footed, pot-bellied, obsidian-black
wash pot, where a good farmer stirs
around in the boiling water
with battling stick, stopping now
and then to offer his delicacies cooling
in the red Dixie cup on the make-shift
tailgate table beside him. But this autumn
we celebrate a different kind of harvest
under a different sky. Tomorrow,
we tie balloons to the hospital bed rail,
eat your favorite cake frosted with butter
and cream cheese, and drink from red
Dixie cups to celebrate your new birthday—
to revel in the kindness of a stranger
somewhere in the world.

Freefall

—after Mark Nepo

Fear wastes air, the poet said,
and he knew. His leukemia-ridden body
knew. But what do you do with it?
Hide it under a bushel? Snuff it out
like you would a candle's wick?
Pound it flat like a thin-tossed pizza
dough? Maybe you drown it with sorrow
or with a good stiff drink or with total
immersion in work. Perhaps, just perhaps—
the answer lies in love.

Lines Written in UAB's Bone Marrow Transplant Unit, 8423

—with lines from the masters and with help from my daughter

How do days hold moments pregnant with both love and fear?

The poet's words providing anchor and resolve—*what stuff 'tis made of [sorrow], whereof it is born, I am to learn*

Posters of family puttied on grey walls. A reveling in four-year-old's confident talk at yesterday's soccer practice—"My body is made for this."

Hope, feathering like thistledown in spring and summer. Love, in sickness and in health

Tracking your cheek on transplant day, a single tear

The poet's words floating about like the birthday balloon in the room—*today it feels so simple, we are here to take care of each other*

Hiccups, relentless, unappeased

I can do all things through Christ. But the transplant doctor? The donor? And how about me? Your faith, bigger than the mustard seed

The magnetism is strong. But my north is your north. I get too close. I push back.

Hide hair, show hair, thin hair, no hair,
Brown hair, blue hair, straight hair, new hair.
Will the hair come back red, mam?
It could come back black as the night, sir.

The poet's words framed in gold on the window sill—*on every tree and bush, millions of small green hands, applauding your return.*

Donor cells, like a school of tiny fish, swimming swiftly towards their new reef

The poet's words rocketing the spirit—*how could anything ever get in the way of generosity?*

A bag of wheat-colored, gouache-like substance suspended from IV pole's horned hook, its tail threading life through a tiny hole in your chest

Your body is made for this.

Fatigue grabbing hold like a pair of vise grip pliers, teeth ground down and hardened for tight squeeze

You will come back.

What if the ancillary new cells do not appear in the bone marrow? The plant does not plant? Your laughter leaves?

Sanctuary

It was her holy place, the front porch.
You could find her there early morning
or late afternoon, meditating on scripture

or throughout the day shelling a mess
of speckled butter beans or silking a tub
of Silver Queen or peeling a dishpan full

of luscious, blushing tomatoes. She kept
the place immaculate, too, performing daily
rituals of clearing away the pecan tree's yellow,

worm-like catkins in springtime, its crunchy,
showy leaves in the fall, and feeding and abluting
the baskets of pink, dragon-winged begonias,

purple-veined petunias, and full-berried asparagus
ferns hanging from the porch's eaves. Never
any cobwebs or storm's debris under her

freshly-painted, cassock-red, rocking chairs,
nor in the not-so-long-ago scoured window sills.
In her eighties when she could no longer adhere

to her daily observances, she sat ecclesiastically
in her rocker, studying the purple martin building
its nest atop the porch's column and communing

with the red birds and thrashers darting from tree
to tree. Twenty years later, I am taking up her
mantle. At seventy, I am learning to speak birdsong.

Winter

Juxtaposition

—after Gerard Manley Hopkins

We praise the beautiful, the lovely, the kind. We love
those who love us back, that which pays homage
to our place in the universe. Red geraniums in clay
pots, razzle-dazzle sunsets, babies, the silence
of stars. We celebrate Holstein Heifers grazing
in green fields, rivers, rushing and strong,
little brooks babbling to the boulders as they trickle by.
We glory in pelicans and herons, the red-tailed hawk
and barn swallows, and hold holy the salmon swimming
upstream to spawn and die. But how about the scorpion
skittering about the desert flexing its pinchers of steel?
The mountain-climbing goat with cloven hooves? The pot
in pieces scattered on the ground, flowers bruised and
broken? Are we at peace with the dung beetle pushing,
straining, to heft two hundred times its body weight?
With a bloat of hippos, bodies like barrels, teeth, long and
sharp, like pointed words? Do we consider wintery skies
and bullfrogs, the forgotten, the lost? Oh, the mickle joy
awaiting us in the fickle, the spare, the strange!

Old Coffers,

—in memory of Hollis, Dan and Bruce, brothers serving in WWII

mildewed and musty, divulging the dead's secrets and
war's wounds and youth's aspirations for glory, adulthood set
in motion—notices to report for duty and maps for the journey

to band with brothers and dog tags and medals and insignias;
coffers, disclosing missives from Hawaii reporting on
the battery's training, jungle and amphibious, and on flowers

as bountiful as Main Street's gossip; coffers revealing
correspondence from England where soldiers' swagger
melts maidens' hearts and where there is talk

of the mighty bomb, its residue as consequential as Pentecost;
coffers displaying letters neatly opened along flap's fold, records
of brothers on the battlefield musing on Mama's mayhaw jelly

atop her hot, tender biscuits, on their quarters where soldiers battle
typhoons and mud and dysentery and rats, on the enemy's demise
in mass at the bottom of a cliff. Coffers, housing war and baring

lives, where memory lingers like the stench of a fisherman's wharf
and looms like an ill-formed rooster tattoo.

Eye-Openers

I.

Beauty is in the eye
of the beholder—behold
the bluebird and the slug!

II.

Elton sang of blue eyes—I sing
of your dancing browns, heavily lashed
and large, melting me like marshmallows
at campfire.

III.

It's said it is easier for a camel to go through
a needle's eye than for a rich man to enter
into the kingdom of heaven—by what implement,
then, do we other mortals measure our chances?

IV.

In the animal world, the horned lizard shoots
blood darts at its predator through its peepers—
when you are wronged these days, I become
the horned lizard.

V.

The story goes that the eye can bewitch
and enchant or inflict discomfort and pain
with just one glance—mamas and children
give witness to this phenomenon.

VI.

The Bard declared the eye of heaven burns
at times too hot—but today it's winter.

VII.

Faith—believing without seeing, trusting without
feeling the nail prints, convinced without touching
the scars.

VIII.

How do political parties appear to see things
so clearly—yet know not which direction
to go?

IX.

The eye can process images viewed
for as little as thirteen milliseconds and see
stars millions of light years away, so—
can I guarantee it to hold you
in its lens for eternity?

X.

We don't always see in black and white—
sometimes the image is clouded in maybe.

XI.

An eye for an eye—
but then what?

XII.

Muscles that control the eyes are the most active
in the body. Don't be confused, though—
the tongue's are stronger.

XIII.

Eye-opener—you are twenty-one
and have a lifetime to live with your love,
and snap, it's over.

Marrow and Mutation

—a duplex after Jericho Brown

We've got today, but again, maybe not—
maybe just this minute, this breath, this right-now song.

Why, then, not belt it, this right-now song, this minute,
    while we yet breathe?
Let us skip and turn and lift and jump, arms outstretched
    in exultation,

arms outstretched to shout with the universe that we exult
    in the now,
the unexpected, the broken and the whole,

the unexpected that sometimes attempts to break us
    or send us spiraling
into the avalanche's path or into the abyss's darkness
    like the news we received yesterday,

news of stem cells in the dark recesses of bone marrow
    growing abysmally
out of control, scarring and causing genetic mutations;

yet when life mutates and we lose control, the very marrow
    of our being
hints of our short stay in this broken but beautiful world
    whispering

of the One who has set eternity in the human heart.
Yes, we've got today—but again, maybe not.

Tilt-o-Whirl World

Five decades ago, there you were
in the student center, twenty-one,
a beautiful, smiling specimen of mischief
and joy, your shoulder-length rufescent locks,
wavey, like a stylish, folding hand-fan,
your mustache ornamenting your six-and-
a-half foot frame like the winged helmet
decorated Hermes. Today, waiting for news
of the donor who will give you back your life,
you still retain those classic good looks
though your hair is less colorful, your mustache
less bold. They turn too fast, these waning days,
yet in the spin, oft times dizzying and dark,
are moments wondrous, miraculous, like birth.

Witnesses

—after Caravaggio's The Raising of Lazarus *(Italy) 1609*

In this winter of woe, I went looking for hope
and found it in the purple pansy's fight for life, in
the maple leaf's ice crystals, illumined by the sun.
I discovered it in the spider's long web, the cricket's
loud chirp, the bluebell's sweet swansong. I saw it
in the ravens' twice-daily care package to the prophet
of old and in today's experimental drug designed
for disease difficult and rare, rare like the white
peacock in the grasslands of Australia. I witnessed
it in the rhythm of the rain, in the salmon's epic journey
to spawn and die, in strangers' fist and elbow bumps,
in their smiles and good wishes. And I heard it
in the instructions at a Bethany burial site
over two thousand years ago—*unbind him
and let him loose.*

Because Life Is So Full of Music—I Shall Dance

the protest of verbena in minor key at November's first frost
a grandchild's first words—Da Da, yo-gurttt, ball—and later
    the crack of his bat and the loud, lone cheers of his mother
butter sizzling in frying pan, making ready the egg
wagon wheels creaking on the rhododendron-filled mountain trail,
    the creek rushing along the purple path
the smoky sound of the saxophone on a street corner at dusk
crickets and bullfrogs and cicadas in the swamp, the occasional
    gurgle and burp of the bog
Shakespeare reverberating across four centuries, his
    characters' whispers and cries of passion, their rants
    and blusters, their dying sighs
an aging man in wheelchair muttering to himself and then breaking
    out in *Gonna take a sentimental journey, gonna set my*
    heart at ease
the rustling hush of angel wings
a ski slope in the Alps, its snow the consistency of wet cement
    roaring to the bottom of a ravine; the stillness that follows
the silence of one's listening
my love's transplant coordinator with tongue grinning
    telephoning with the news of a bone marrow match

Master Class

He introduced you to nature. In early morning,
in late afternoon, in sunshine or gray skies, he
extended your tiny hand to meet the pine.
Tree, he would say, placing your fingers
on the bark, *this is a tree. Flower,* he would add,
cradling the lemony-scented rhododendron
to your face. *Purty flower. Pur-ty.* And you
reached out your tiny hands and leapt and
jumped and shrieked and cooed, your whole
world a wonder.

Years later, he coached you for hours after school
on the monkey bars to allay your fears about
the upcoming presidential fitness test percolating
in your perfectionist, seven-year-old mind.
As you grew, he taught you the difference
in a Phillips' head and flathead when assembling
Barbie and Ken's Malibu dreamhouse or when
adjusting a carburetor on a Briggs and Stratton
lawn mower. He coached you in packing the car
for the beach, teaching that even a toothpick takes up
space. He instructed you to listen with your skin
to the stories of your grandmothers. He gave
you lessons in driving the stick-shifting,
imperial-red Dodge Avenger he bought you
at fifteen and then gave advice regarding boys
and strangers, advising you to pass on those
who would do you harm.

Today, some forty years later, he is still
in the classroom though the class is less
interactive as you cradle his arm in yours to begin
the slow, arduous laps about the transplant unit.
His growing smile reveals his satisfaction
in completing the task as difficult as fighting
fire-breathing bulls in a field of dragons' teeth
and his pride in knowing the student has become
the master.

After November Frost

she would gather the leafy greens
in the kitchen sink under the running water
to remove grit and gunge. Then she
would tenderly strip the leaves from the stalks
and cube the bulbous, purple-tinged, dingy-
white shapes for the boiling ham-hocked or
streak-o'leaned broth on the stove. I loved
seeing her there, loved hearing my mother
explain how the first frost on turnips makes them
less bitter, loved her hands brimming
the five-gallon pot with the greens, allowing
the rolling water to shrink the leaves.

Making Candy in December

—to Mops, with love

How we worked together back then
in the tiny kitchen at the rear of the house,
one of us bringing sugar, water and syrup
to a slow boil, stirring the silvery-white
liquid once or twice as it thickened,
the other beating egg whites with a smidgen
of salt and vanilla, stiffening them like our starched
and ironed Sunday dresses. The one at the stove
intermittently lifted and tilted the syrup-covered
wooden spoon into the air to determine
if the confection threaded toward the pot immersed
in the water-filled, cast-iron skillet. To ensure
the mixture was just the right hardness to pour
into the whipped eggs, she further tested it
by allowing a single drop into a cup of cool water,
anticipating a clear tiny rock in the bottom of the container.
If the formation appeared, she gave warning for her sibling
to make ready, to scurry to give the eggs one last spin
before pouring the seething bubbles into the frothy
snow. Together we watched the two mixtures form
a rolling volcano climbing the sides of bowl and then
took turns stirring, sometimes walking outside to give
a few more whirls with the spoon and to allow
December's nip to hasten the cooling. Finally,
when the candy had lost its gloss and was ready
to drop onto the waxed and waiting paper, we grabbed
teaspoons and made art, beautifully-formed glistening
mountains, up and down the wax-papered countertop.

O, to share more candy Christmases!
To wrap and ribbon for others. To give it all away.

Christmas Across the Years

The heart is a repository of vanished things.
—Mark Doty

A first doll—
One with a broken face
But one she could afford

Oranges, studded with cloves—
Amongst cedar clippings
In pink depression glass

Through the wall's cracks
Blinking yellows, reds and Gatsby greens—
A family's first Christmas lights

In the bed of rusty International truck
A family—scouring rutted roads
For perfect pine

A gathering about the old Baldwin upright
Leaning in for verse's third stanza lyrics—eleven
Voices breaking the sound barrier in clamor and song

The 5 and 10's bins of orange slices,
Chocolate-covered creams and bonbons
Yellow, pink, and white—eyes hungering

For the child, a tiny red bottle
Of perfumed water—
Stowed 'til Christmas morning

Wind and hound dogs howling
Bare light bulbs flickering—
Keeping time with the rain on tin roof

Gumdrops, red and green, attached
To dry, broken limb planted
In coffee can—a taste of enchantment
'Twas the night before Christmas—
Though *Sandy Claus* was not officially invited,
Neither was he denied

Amongst conifer's cones and branches
And waxy-red candles—the oversized red-lettered
Family Bible open to Luke's gospel

A fatigued farming father with unexpected energy
Sharing the Christmas story—
And the glory of the Lord shown round about

Ode to the Fruitcake

—with line from Truman Capote

O, beautiful round of sweetness!
O, satisfying work of art fashioned
with red and green candied cherries and
golden pineapple, glazed, translucent!
You have sustained us through
the centuries with your plump,
juicy raisins and your meaty, freshly-
hulled pecans laced with butter and
infused with nutmeg and cinnamon
and other spices. Yet some have branded
you a culinary punching bag providing
holiday humor to the masses. Late night
comedy has derided you and injured
your reputation, quipping you're the gift
that goes on giving, much like the white
elephant nobody treasures. But O, sacred,
delectable indulgence, those naysayers
have not been privy to the joyous face
of one looking upon you with wonder,
exclaiming, *Now, that's a precious
memory,* proceeding then to recount
the story of a Christmas-aproned mama
unveiling a cheesebox-sized you, a mound
of mouth-watering flavor, a you, aged
with a fruit-of-the-vine red liquid or better
yet, with a rare, clear elixir, bootleg
quality.

O, taste of heaven, we bow to
your goodness once more and ask
your forgiveness for the folly and fatuity
of fools, for even now some of us mortals
are looking to yet another season of crisp
and cool weather when we will exclaim

with the generations of yesterday, *Oh my,
it's fruitcake weather.*

Family Gathering, December 17, 2022

Loss is nothing else but change, and change is Nature's delight.
—Marcus Aurelius.

We feel the loss in the dying
year, in the holidays' festivities.
Though our gathering still looms loud
and large—cooing babes, whimpering
puppies and bold fashion—since you left
in the spring, Sister, there is an absence
in the banter of the house, in the leaves-
laden pool outside the picture window,
in the yard's free-standing firepit void
of warmth and glow and indigo flames.
Yet we do not languish long, for we have
our stories, stories of Christmases past,
documented in your umpteen spiral-bound books
of black and white and sepia-toned photos snapped
with the large-eyed 35 mm Cannon always
about your neck. Of family's oft-times
heated and passionate discussions about what
it means to love, of the brilliant red bird in black
mask and bright top hat at work in our winters,
making pliable the twigs for her nest
in the evergreen.

I Walk the Path

this unseasonably-warm New Year's Day
and see a woman on park bench with Great Dane
and Great Pyrenees posing for picture; two boys,

stepping gingerly into mud puddles, then splashing
each other, then submerging themselves, their parents
on cellphones, clueless as to their children's world,

perhaps clueless as to their own; a teen jumping
rope, his Nikes screeching like a rose-breasted
grosbeak; a princess pedaling her pink tricycle;

and finally, remnants of Christmas just days ago—
a wreath, a string of lights, a deflated Santa,
a mailbox's big bow. And while the weather is

as welcoming as ripened kumquats on the tree
in springtime, dark clouds gather on the horizon
and squirrels scurry to their nests in the threadbare

oaks, and emails ding out yet another dooms-day
message of Omicron, reminding us winter will still
have its say. Yet, we despair not when muskrats burrow

high upon the river's banks and halos frequent
about the sun and the moon, for hibernation bespeaks
of rest and new life, and the robin's migration brings

a yearning for its song.

On Andrew Wyeth's *Public Sale,* 1943

An old farmer forced to sell the place
after his wife's long illness. It's just as well—
the land had grown sick, too, the ochre hills
now whispering of death, the near-bare trees
lisping loss, the graying sky sighing
with sorrow.

Just off the dirt road leading to the house,
people swarming like crickets, scavenging
through barrels and baskets and harvesters
and ploughs for bargains, steals and giveaways.
The old pick-up truck, having hauled many
a load of wood and livestock and grain,
now sits rusty, no life in its bed, only traces
of sun-kissed blueberries and silken stalks
of corn and golden-red kindling for the fire
that must have raged tenderly just inside
the clapboard building where cast-iron pot
atop cold furnace still invites the fire.
Which objects bespeak life in this
solitary place? The husked, seed corn
roped across barn rafters, the hollowed-out
bread trough on rough, log-hewn kitchen
table, the faded blue apron thrown over nail
on cedar-paneled wall? What of hand-
crafted baby crib, a yellowing christening
gown and cobwebs its only décor?
The enameled bedpan at the foot
of four-poster bed, now a nesting berth
for rats and lizards and other critters?
What will witness of life? What will testify
in silence to love? For *while the earth
remains, seedtime and harvest, cold and heat,
summer and winter, day and night shall not cease.*

Déjà Vu

Perhaps it is the smell of a burning field
that takes me back to the springs of childhood,

my father preparing to plant, to turn over the soil
for the new seeds and a new start. Maybe it's ginseng

or peppermint or lemon lozenges that call up mid-winter
croups when he coaxed me to swallow a half-spoon

of Mentholatum or Vicks Salve to soothe my sore throat
or to rid me of my barking cough. It could be the smell

of Old Spice that transports me to the tiny white, taper-lit
church in December, I on his arm, feeling special that I am

the first and only sibling to have had the honor of his giveaway,
the lingering aftershave on my cheek the guarantee he was

there over fifty years ago. Maybe it is the several bundles
of kindling stacked neatly on the hearth or the scent

of turpentine from the burning pine affirming he is gone.

Truth and Beauty

—after Ted Kooser and John Keats

They were artsy, people of culture,
say the Lenox limited edition Boehm birds
nesting in the book cases and Butler Brown's
muted barns and abandoned farmhouses
on the long, dark-paneled wall housing
off-white couch and worn pillows;
educated and well-traveled say stacks
of *National Geographics,* the Bible
in German, and the bookoodles of photo
albums inside end tables and behind
glassed wall cabinets; for sure, they were
keepers of time, for here a clock, there a clock,
everywhere, a tick-tock—plastic, wooden,
ceramic, and tin. Mantle clocks, table clocks,
large and small. Grandfather clocks swallowing
foyers and eating up tight spaces. Cuckoos
with weighted pine-cone chains inviting
a once-a-day pull to encourage a little red bird
to spring forward on the hour and half hour.
A woman lived there say living room's low-
backed Victorian loveseat with dusty-pink
roses, say the White Diamonds body powder
on the night table at the side of the bed.
A man, too, say the heavy rubber boots
and the metal dog tags and the miniature car
collection on shelves built for its display.

But something had changed, say the beautifully
designed flower gardens whose fish pools
and water lilies, elephant ears and statues lay
stagnant, broken, and overrun with weeds.
Life happened say the porch's sagging eaves,
the heavy leg brace lying beside the leather recliner,
arm and leg rests picked and stretched and worn
like a sweater ready for discard. Time abandoned
them say the pieces that once warmed the house
with gongs and chimes and cuckoos.

The Working Dead

At twilight the dead begin
their nocturnal habits
of cutting and hauling logs,

noisying it up, perhaps
that we'll go looking
to relieve them

of their back-breaking work
and the icy winds biting
at their souls. Some acknowledge

us and go on sawing as if on
the clock, timed, the job expiring
at the crow of the cock,

while others sit a spell
in the shadows of the warm fire
allowing questions and then answering

in their watery-thin language of blinks
and nods and slip-and-slide smiles.
Do they worry about us?

Are they concerned about erasure?
Ours or theirs?
Do they laugh with us

or at us—at our indulgences,
our obsessions, our follies and our gaffes?
When will they rest by the river?

Meanwhile, the work goes on—
the dead go on living,
and we keep on dying

Awaiting the Phoebe's Song

Scattered throughout my sister's house,
her collection of Boehm birds. Plates,
singles and groupings, adding a whiff

of color to the mahogany bookcases,
a fleck of light to the dark paneled
walls. She had gathered the limited

edition over the years, had invested
in its timelessness and beauty so that
in the bleak winter she might see

the cardinal's red crest in clusters
of imperial-purple grapes, hear
the golden crowned kinglet in bearded

blue iris, graceful and tall. Today,
as I stack and restack her plates in the curio
by my own hearth, winter's winds are

whipping down the alleyway, and
the streets are quiet, except for occasional call
of fire and other rescue services. But in this

winter, I am the one hunkering down in the cold
awaiting the phoebe's song.

The Heart

—after Danusha Laméris and Ted Hughes

The heart is not a gate.
A door that opens and closes
at one's will. Not automated.
Not smartphone-controlled. It is
not a soft start and stop and
could even develop jerks and skips
and flutters over time. It comes
with no guarantee, and the warning
is clear—whatever happens there,
happens.

To Come to Naught

At last, everything becomes
a whisper. The dew disappears
as it meets the day, and grass
withers as summer turns toward
fall. The daffodil in vogue
in early spring becomes warm
weather's dying dance. Fame
and glory fade like red pigment
in the scorching, noon-day sun
as empires crumble and dictators
fall and Wisdom whispers, *Vanity,
vanity, all is vanity.* Yet we press on.
In sorrow and in song we press on.
For that is what it means to live—
that is the journey to joy.

On Suffering

—after sermon by Dr. Cody McNutt, 2022

On the road of suffering
upon which we are destined
to travel, help me to suffer well.
I pray I not overwhelm my brother
and sister with incessant chatter
about the road's rigors and rues but live
that I invite a curiosity about what
is gained through pain, a curiosity
like a few-weeks baby intrigued
by its mother's smile. I want winter's worry
and discontent burned away that happiness
flourish like April's Mason bees emerging
from the woodpecker's hole to taste
the garden's gold. Grant that I suffer
well on the journey and at journey's end,
die well. To suffer and die well.
Be it so, Lord, be it so.

The Life-Giver

—after Thomas Lux

opens the door of the world to dawn's alpenglow
and closes it to starlings' murmurations at winter's dusk.

The Life-giver douses fields with buttercups and swells
forests with evergreens. The Life-giver battens down

winds and causes oceans to recoil. He sends downbursts and gentle
rains to replenish the parched earth, seasoning it with petrichor

and garnishing it with rainbows. He renders his creation a right
smart of play and display—from ostrich's wild run to peacock's

colorful exhibit to cheetah's long sprint to flamingo's single-leg
balancing act. When you go for elective surgery only to find you

have life-altering cancer yet learn days later it is non-invasive and
low-grade, the Life-giver brought it to pass! Also, the accident

that thrust life-changing physical alterations upon you
but introduced you to the nurse who would love you a lifetime.

You escaped death by an inch? Or a mile? By a second? A decade?
Again, the Life-giver's mercies, new every morning. Let us praise

the Life-giver for swallows' nests in eaves of houses, for children's
laughter, for the blood coursing our veins.

Amen.

Evening

Life is a shadow diminishing at day's end,
shrinking, reconciling, making peace with its twin.

It is Wyeth's Christina running wildly in golden fields of grain
panting, reaching, collapsing in exhaustion and praise.

Life is a Kodak's perfect winter sunset, the intense oranges and
reds cascading over an old farmhouse; it is the slamming

of the screened back door. Life is a gamer folding after observing
his losing hand; it's his bluffing his way to a win, playing

the deck to the last card. Life is Gabriel dusting off his gig bag,
positioning himself for trumpet's final blast—

long, metallic, certain—like evening.

Now

We know this is no mere moment, however brief.
—Robert Penn Warren

An early-October evening, the sun blooming
with begonia pinks and bittersweet reds, easing
behind the oak and evergreens; a squirrel darting
up the yellowing maple's trunk; a blue jay,
teasing, as he flits a little higher in the branches
enjoying, perhaps, his last fling before winter.
The crepe myrtle's crimson blossoms inking
the ground and the single black-eyed Susan
whispering, *Come a little closer. Get to know me
before I go.* Resurrection flowers, long and tall,
little red miracles astounding in near-bare beds,
encouraging the moment, inviting us to linger,
to take their slender stalks in hand, to hold and
behold their spidery blooms, to imprint their glory
on the heart for winter.

Behold!

Beauty and happiness come! Unexpectedly
in the single seconds that make up our days.
They come as two mourning doves umbrellaing
together under the branches of the lacy, tea-green
cypress fern outside the rain-flecked window.
They come as the Japanese Beetle, its metallic-blue
and green head, its copper-colored back and tan
wings, almost hidden in the rose bush confiscated
from our mother's garden. They come in the sun's
slant in mid-afternoon. In a deceased sister's succulents
surviving the winter's hard freeze. In baby's breath.
They come to one awaiting a bone marrow transplant,
to his spouse of forty-nine years packing for the one
hundred days away from home in the city of steel
and strangers. They come to the refugee fleeing
her birth country, a brimming paper bag and walking
cane her only possessions.

Proclamations in Fire and Ice

—Iceland, 2017

You have taken me to a remote place
to proclaim your glory, untamed, palatial,
everlasting, and holy. I see you in cascading
waters, steep cliffs, deep gorges and lasting
sunsets. In skies wild with aurora's dancing
waves. In the hot springs, steaming
like a coolant in overheated engine. I hear you
in the quiet rivers and lakes, in the shallow
lagoons, in the mad and manic geysers' spews.
I feel you in electric-blue icecaps carving out valleys
and narrow fjords, in the katabatic winds playing
over ice at evening. Towering crags and mighty
monoliths testify of You, and here my feeble voice
joins Nature's throng of bold and manifold witnesses.

Come before Winter,

before the snowy owl arrives
and waterfowl depart, before the rabbit
changes color and the black bear slows
heart; before interlocking vines hang
naked from near-barren trees and
the ground mutes itself with browns
and grays and smokey griefs; before
the holly waxes its leaves and before
its berries grow madder than the blood
of saints; before the hair grows thick
on oxen's necks and storms brew
their offspring in deep waters. Come
quickly. Before the cold. Before
the shadow.

About the Author

Jo Taylor was born in rural Middle Georgia in the fifties, the seventh of nine children. After graduating from the University of Georgia in 1976 with a BA in English, she taught high school English for thirty-five years. Today she lives in Covington, Georgia, with her husband, enjoying writing poetry, taking online poetry classes, and visiting with her two grandsons in Alabama. She self-published her first collection of poems, *Strange Fire,* in 2021.